This Book Belongs To

Made in the USA
Monee, IL
20 August 2021

76135245R00069